Face to Face

Also by Adrian Lane and published by Ginninderra Press
Southpaw

Adrian Lane

Face to Face

Acknowledgements

With great thanks to all who have contributed
to the development of this collection

All proceeds from the collection and associated readings will be
used to support the indigenous Greenlandic church and students
from countries of the former Yugoslavia studying at the Evangelical
Theological Seminary in Osijek, Croatia (www.evtos.hr).

Face to Face
ISBN 978 1 76041 174 9
Copyright © text Adrian Lane 2016
Cover photo (Perast Village and Kotor Bay, Montenegro) © ollirg

First published 2016 by
GINNINDERRA PRESS
PO Box 3461 Port Adelaide SA 5015
www.ginninderrapress.com.au

Contents

New Zealand Trio	11
I Kids Fishing, Days Bay, Wellington	11
II Cooking on a Candle, Christchurch, January 2011	12
III Stills from a Restaurant Window, Wellington	13
Cars: The New Cigarettes	14
Sorting Books	15
The Oslo Boat	16
I Moving Still	16
II Bedtime	16
III We're Moving Still	17
Vigeland Park Sculptures	18
The Scream: Lament for Edvard Munch	19
Herceg-Novi Suite	21
I Bay of Kotor	21
II Trajekt Kamenari (Kamenari Ferry)	22
III Noisy Night Sea	24
IV The Bronze Grasshopper	25
V New Men	26
VI The Night Winds Down	27
VII Season's End	28
Capital Pleasures	29
The Berm	30
Perth Airport Bus: QF 1648 Paraburdoo	31
A Very Private Pain	32
On Disappointment	34
Honour	35
Mothers and Sons	36
On Being Old	37
Drysdale Christmas	38
Parrots in the Pears	40

Glen Ayr, Pokolbin	42
Falling in Love with Queensland	44
Rock Climbing	47
A Man's Frown	48
Doha, Qatar	49
Trocadero Gardens, Paris	50
iBagel, Copenhagen	51
Somewhere over Turkey	52
Herceg-Novi Summer Suite	53
I A Man's World	53
II The Passing Parade…	55
III At Kamenari: Olympics 2012	57
IV Water Polo Training: Montenegro Juniors	58
V In the Garden Restoran, Perast	59
VI Day Trip to Žanjic	60
VII The Ballet on the Bay	62
VIII You're Never Sure or Nobody Speaks English	64
At the British Museum	67
Lament for Podgorica: Isaiah 55	68
Rendition: On Hearing News of American Torture	69
Esther	70
King for King	71
Be Strong and Courageous	72
Greenland Quartet	74
I Attiak Ittuk crosses the Arctic Circle	74
II Morning, Attiak Ittuk	75
III Sailing with Icebergs, Eki Glacier	76
IV With an Amazing View	77
Tromsø Quartet	78
I View from a Hotel Window, Tromsø	78
II The Cloudy Finger	79
III Crossing the Bridge	80

IV Through Famine and Fire	81
Trio: Return to Oslo	82
I Oslofjord, Early Morning	82
II View from a Breakfast Window, Oslo	83
III Vigeland Park Revisited: Summer Evening	84

for friends and family
who sustain and delight

> Now we see but a poor reflection as in a mirror;
> then we shall see face to face.
> 1 Corinthians 13:12

New Zealand Trio

I Kids Fishing, Days Bay, Wellington

Through bitter wind they plunge into the chill
Tear mussels from the algaed piers, and rise
Grinning
Piling their treasures on lapping edge
Then race glistening up slippery steps
To dive again.

Hopping, dancing, in the freeze
Shivering
With slaked hair and arms abreast
They rock-split their cache with practised skill,
Bait their hooks and cast – oblivious to eye –
Brimming with delight
As they land their taut line gleaming
Silver flapping on wharf's end.

II Cooking on a Candle, Christchurch, January 2011

I knew at once my stay would not be long.
It was empty –
Not a summer holiday empty –
But an eerie, 'things are worse than they seem' empty.

Turning left, my way was barred by fences guarding piles of rubble
And here's another, and another
Demolition cranes, cones across the street
Crossless churches, leaning on steel
A sorry note from the manager
A hotel cooking on a candle
Headquarters with plywood windows and a wheelbarrow inside
Vacated.

The bed shudders.
Not a surging, swinging shake –
Just a settling, falling-into-place shake –
At least, that's what I tell myself
From the 21st floor.

III Stills from a Restaurant Window, Wellington

Silver light neath storm clouds makes the white hulls shine,
    masts too
The car carrier sits behind like a huge Beluga whale
The birds screech and flee
The cat to Days Bay passes below, in miniature, its rear foaming
The gale flaps taut the banners of Te Papa
and the trees shake hard in the salty wind
and the first splats pelt the window
like gravel from an angry hand.

After the rain, figures grab their gaberdines
and race across the slaked black tar
The air smells crisp and clean
Beyond the chop, headlights flicker round shore's edge:
tiny stars at mountains' foot
While Petone's lights sparkle, bracelet on sea's shore.
And still the wind flaps hard the banners
Rifle-cracking, as the dusk settles dim.

And now, its cobalt blue
with white lights bright round harbour's rim,
before the fog creeps: mouthing,
shimmering the haloes floating in the dark;
before the squall drops its curtain
and hides all –
told only by my cheese
reflected in the glass.

Cars: The New Cigarettes

Cars:
The new cigarettes
Burning resources non-renewable
Choking, killing, maiming
Even those who try to save
By walking, cycling;
Forcing low-density housing,
Massive lots, garages, tar over half the earth,
Stormwater flooding, wasting, guzzling –
You've no idea how much we pay –
Freeways over farms,
Now taking, eating our food
To fuel our little worlds
That push away:
Addicts never know their smell till clean.

The greatest cities in the world:
London, Paris, New York,
All have subways – made great by subways –
Who visits LA?
Everybody loves a tram, a train:
Don't underestimate the power – pain – of gas,
Be careful lest on looking in the rear
You find it gone:
Congestion up ahead.

Sorting Books

Whatever happened to that old *Rag and Bone Pony* book
I was given as a Sunday School prize,
or that *Life of Paul*
for chairing the Latin Reading Competition at Abbotsleigh,
or all those wonderful novels from Aunty Marg
that arrived each birthday and Christmas from Melbourne,
nurturing a late night love for story
under the mosquito nets on the veranda at Paradise?

No doubt painfully pruned in a former cull,
musty and mouldy from the damp at Castle Hill,
provoking sneezes, needing to be aired.

I can't bear discarding these tokens of kindness,
calling up memories, signs of care,
not fully appreciated, understood at the time,
clumsy at their receiving.

It's ironic these prizes waited 40 years to be read on the cusp
 of their disposal –
a life too crowded to enjoy, reflect, savour, know;
only now do they begin to share their treasures –
not in print – they tatter and fall apart the more,
but by their signatures,
of love,
only now beginning to be known.

The Oslo Boat

I Moving Still

It's 11.15.
In the blue light
tankers glide past like models on a pond,
the smiling moon hangs low amongst the clouds,
the engines hum, and the AC streams.

Approaching the guard rail I dare not look
and feel giddy,
as though some unseen force
is set to grab my legs and toss me over.
Kids sit and play in pools perilously close to the edge.
I hastily retreat to safety indoors,
and walk the stairs perfectly.
We're moving still.

II Bedtime

It always seems strange undressing in front of a porthole:
a mixture of naïve exhibitionism and coy reserve,
as though that oil tanker in the other lane
could actually see you –
but it still feels strange.

III We're Moving Still

Twelve stories high, with some extras below,
we glide into the night light,
blue on the longest day,
moving still.

Landed opposite the Opera –
marble white glacier sliding into the sea –
snug inside our hotel rooms,
we're moving still.

Vigeland Park Sculptures

They stand amongst the summer roses, falling water
Massive, tender, strong.
Fathers playwrestle with their children
Mothers nurse their babies at the breast
A grandpa cares.

> Kids run about the statues
> Bursting with smiles
> Giggling at their nakedness

A boy carries his brother on his back
Lovers caress
Two friends sit close, knowing their care.

> Gentle, soft, unweatherable stone
> Crafted to the touching in all its vital story
> This sculpture park of Eden too beautiful to bear
> Yearns for yet another world more solid in its glory.

Vigeland Park is the popular name for Frogner Park, an extensive public park in Oslo, where Gustav Vigeland's lifework of 212 bronze and granite sculptures line its avenues and serve as focal points. Vigeland (1869–1943) was heavily influenced by Vitalism, a Nordic art and social movement during the first decades of the 20th century.

The Scream: Lament for Edvard Munch

Women at once saint and whore
and one unhappily devoted

O Edvard,
child of the praying pair,
pained by a mother's, sister's loss –
did it have to be this way?

O Edvard,
fired by youthful brilliance, under Jægar's spell,
you gamble away your aunt's laboured pennies –
did it have to be this way?

O Edvard,
seduced by the angel whore,
you sit alone, benighted,
melancholy on the beach,
jealous, jilted,
as your common love is ripped away –
did it have to be this way?

O Edvard,
revisiting old sins, old pains, which breakdown lead
the unrepentant prodigal
who fears he'll burn in hell,
ever searching for that vitalism – robust, sensuous,
in glorious bold colours: alive! –
could it have been otherwise?

Now, alone, you live among your paintings and tend the
    vegetables
while the gate lock rusts.
The world now knows and owns your pain,
screaming from a blood-red sky:
if only it were otherwise.

With reference to Edvard Munch, *Melancholy* (oil on canvas, 1891), *The Scream* (oil, tempera and pastel on cardboard, 1893) and *Death in the Sickroom* (oil on canvas, 1895). Superscription from E. Munch, N 30 in Poul Erik Tøjner, *Munch in his own Words* (Prestel, Munich 2003).

Herceg-Novi Suite

I Bay of Kotor

All poems start with a lump in the throat
This lump's the sun, sparkling on crinkled waters
As I draw my morning's curtains –
Bright light: stunning the eyes
Off the blue bay hugged by muscled arms
Thumbnail-tipped at the fort.

What joy for Kotor's sons
These safe peaks to see
Post globes of lonely travel;
What joy the palms,
The rhythmed, rolling waves
On red-roofed, whitewashed shores.

A clipper makes her entry:
Proud and steady – just five sails set
Five-masted, blue and white,
She bejewels this sapphire crown.

This suite was occasioned by time enjoyed at Herzeg-Novi, on the Bay of Kotor, Montenegro. The *Royal Clipper* is the largest full-rigged sailing ship in the world. Inspired by the 1902 German tall ship *Preussen*, she was built in 2000 and currently serves as a cruise ship. Five-masted, her complement of 42 sails covers 56,000 square feet (www.starclippers.com).

II Trajekt Kamenari (Kamenari Ferry)

The bay is really seven
with as many little islands
dotted round its shore.
From Igalo and Herceg
it shoulders Bijela's shipyards –
Tivat's foggy airport is on the other side –
to narrow,
then open
into yet another wondrous world
jewel-boxing cave paintings, Roman ruins,
Risan, Perast, and the ancient walled city of Kotor:
the fortressed hidden harbour
safely coving each empire's pride.

The bay wakes and sleeps
in its daily, nightly rhythms –
across the fjord's narrows
the ferries never sleep.

From Kamenari to Lepetani
they join the windy ribbons
clinging to limestone walls:
Back and forth, back and forth.
Watch the cars race to catch the boat,
their drivers scrambling for tear-off tickets,
hear the tyres clunk as each crosses the ramp –
the regulars parking perfectly,
the uninitiated, well…
Tourists by the tonne, plated and perused,
see the hull drop with every bus and truck –
it looks easy – loading, unloading,
'But if this baby isn't balanced,
we'll spill or even spew.'

The deckhands in orange uniforms laugh and greet their friends.
One brings coffee in demitasse cups
trayed from the café beside.
All captains in this world – they know the globe,
practical men –
look as they loose the hawsers with a flick,
raise the gangway, place the Stop.
The engine rumbles –
feel the swirl as the stern sinks in:
another crossing, another coast.
Heart of the bay: bay of my heart.

III Noisy Night Sea

Lights rim the bay,
Studded by four lonely fishing boats.
Rolling white fuses run 'long hidden borders,
Bursting,
To spill in pouring fountains
Cross concrete ledges
Not long left by bathers;
Dumping, snorting,
Frothing in freezing cauldrons –
Umbrella boys race in shadows to clear away the chairs –
Crashing, smashing, sucking
Trucks of crunching pebbles:
Is this an angry sea,
Or just glad to stretch and yawn?

Yet it is soothing, settling
And will quieten at tide's ebb,
To leave a salty freshness
Steaming clean tomorrow's dawn.

IV The Bronze Grasshopper

Good-looker,
Loping lithe in orange boardies – almost surly,
Long-legged, long-armed, long-backed,
Dupain-like,
Adjusting, scratching, checking his skin in the sun,
He plays his toes through the water,
Splashes to cool himself,
Dives
And shakes his head as he showers.

Body-conscious
He makes faces at the girls,
Splays himself prone
On the warm whitewashed wall,
Runs his hands through his hair,
Cross his chest –
A bronze grasshopper,
Not even half aware
Of all that he oozes.

Max Dupain is an Australian photographer best known for his iconic images of swimmers and sunbathers.

Boardies: board shorts – a kind of surfwear.

V New Men

What fire will fuse this strength, these sons?
Athleticism delights,
Some may soldiering choose –
But soldier for what?
Self's appetites reward,
Yet leave one searching more:
Legend must be left –
But what will legend be?
Family for many, a cause or craft for some,
Others the mind or art – what will stir and feed?
Unless it be heaven's joys, hollow it will seem,
Heaven's joys outlast, and give all others reason:
So how to heaven these hearts
Is my prayer to come,
For when these hearts are heavened,
My wrestling will be won.

VI The Night Winds Down

Again the haze has come.
Moonshine lights the shorepath
and glints on crêpe waters.
The sea is still,
lapping only when one listens.
A cat surveys the jump cross decks
lolling in the harbour.

A fishing boat returns,
trays full of silver sparkle.
Three youths argue the price of mussels.
A salty freshness fills the air.
The lighthouse flashes,
Oldies dance to country blues –
The night winds down.

Stallholders pack their panelled kiosks,
A few late drinkers enjoy quiet company,
The soccer plays silently on the hotel screen,
Couples wander,
A local cycles home,
Waiters stack the tables,
lock the bollards.
A motorbike noises the air.
The night winds down.
The night winds down.

VII Season's End

Excitement at the rail:
in the dark and noisy night
a fishing boat,
ripped from its mooring,
is flung through the surf
to crash land on the shore,
only to be seized again,
swallowed in the swirl.

The swimming bu'oys, also torn,
bob about the foam –
white balls knotted top a rolling sea,
midst beach chairs in the churn.

The dawn has come:
the sea still roars –
long sleeves, long pants today;
the boat is smashed –
though tethered now –
concrete anchors spill the beach
'mongst plastic bottles, wooden joists,
heaved on the pebbled cove.

The owner hurries to wind in flapping awnings.
Waiters plan time with their northern girlfriends,
stack the chairs.
Rain makes new sounds on the roof,
through the drains.
Summer's over. Season's over. Summer's end.

Herceg-Novi, Montenegro, September–October 2009.

Capital Pleasures

Sculpture Garden, National Gallery of Australia, Canberra

Flaming helmets zoom smooth along the hidden bike-path
from left, from right, from left again
giant ladybirds
red, white, black
mohawk spiked against the magpies
headless
ducks on a shooting range.

Bobbing baseball caps jogging
glimpses of muscle shirts
wide-brimmed shades of agèd ladies
taking their daily,
brushed-back perms of Hawke-ish oldies
showing off their hair.

I sit among the sculptures,
Bible in hand,
a stage of lake and trees, framed.
Rhythmic paddles dance on cool waters,
the bunting of the tourist boat flutters in the breeze,
voices carry over the water
through carillon carols, magpies in trees.
Crafted buildings in the distance
nestle on the slopes of contoured hills:
Architects built this city, with art
and tell amidst our blindness
of a beauty oft forgot.

The Berm

O lowly berm
whose very name unknown
belies your earthly use.
Floods, din and crash thou dost repel
and even beautify
if pleasantly planted
A home for birds and insects bright –
yet who would know?
Hidden
from our sight.

Berm: a raised shoulder or hillock alongside a road.

Perth Airport Bus: QF 1648 Paraburdoo

Men
Heaps of men
Bearded, unshaved
With sunnies and caps
Joking, chatting, greeting
Shorts and hairy legs
Thongs
Tatts
Just glad to be with each other
Men

QF 1648 is a Qantas charter mainly used by fly in, fly out miners travelling to the remote iron ore mining towns of Paraburdoo and Tom Price in the Pilbara region of north-west Western Australia.

A Very Private Pain

In honour of Ben Mulherin (24.8.1985–8.12.2008)

Dear Chris and Lindy,
I wonder if you'd send me a picture
of Ben
when things settle down.
Not on his own –
I never think of him on his own –
but always with Tim
or with his brothers
or with you all –
he was always with people.
I can't imagine the pain of losing
your baby, your little boy
your clunky teenager
your strong son,
but with four brothers
my heart hurts
a very private pain –
hard to know with whom to share –
I dare not burden you, or ask your care,
wrung out in the grieving –
oh wretched pain!
Do you get on with life and somehow dishonour him?
Or always weep?
He, lover of life, would never have you so constrained.
Maturely sad he knows
it can never be the same –
always amputated,
sending messages,

feeling, knowing,
but never whole,
until we join him
on the other side.

On Disappointment

A very private sorrow
of hopes unmade
of dreams untimely woken.
How does one care for broken glass?

This glass has emptied all
and being broke is stepped around
swept
or carefully discarded.

The glass weeps.
May it not with sharpness kill –
which is its wont –
ground down
gone to ground
What'll it be:
clear, green, brown or blue?

Honour

They're quick to clip his wings –
jealousy? A sorrow for self?
Perhaps his light exposes –
so a fear, a cowardice –
or maybe takes the spot off them?
Perhaps they just can't abide his standing,
or stand his abiding:
driven by the word or the world?

Give me grace to love, Lord,
those who, needing light, cannot see
that by giving it away
gain great, fly all.

Mothers and Sons

Prompted by *Oedipus*, Glyn Warren Philpot (oil on canvas, National Gallery of Victoria, 4663-3)

She grips his arm
with blazing eye,
fury in her marble face.

He kneels in penitence below –
what he's done he doesn't know
and pushes as he dare away.

He's her man – she doesn't know
and to another will not give –
but until she's loosed the grasp
can he to another live.

Not till then can he return
standing as a man now grown.
Not till then can she mature
gentle, giving, filled with grace.

On Being Old

Pardon us if we seem a little distracted
But our griefs have collected
And it isn't so easy to put them aside.

Pardon us if we appear rather sober
But our griefs have collected
And it seems disrespectful to put them aside.

Pardon us if we sound somewhat sorry
But our griefs have collected
And we lose all our learnings if we put them aside.

Drysdale Christmas

Hume Highway, NSW

The haze hangs low on the shrouded hills
The grass is dry, crispy and bare
Stock trucks heading south mean trouble up north
And my clothes are hot in the bag.

A truck has rolled on an entry ramp
Smashing its cab rudely like a boxer's face
Tearing its trailers
Tumbling, spewing as the load shifts.
I prayed long and hard for that driver who's probably lost his job
And still owes
Now with no chance of paying off the bank.

Another truck has run out of puff on Conroy's Gap.
It sits stalled in the lane, its hazards flashing.
I pass dead cars with bonnets up
And families with flaking kids pink and puffy
Trying to recover at shadeless rest stops.

The car makes strange noises in the heat
Belts slip and screech, the AC leaks,
All my toiletries have changed consistency
The grass is eaten tight
And the sheep huddle under lone trees
Or by the dam – its water muddy.

The ash of a roadside fire
Acrids my nose,
Its black scar wrecking the fences
And leaving beastly Drysdale logs grimly grinning,
Their dangling roots teasing, taunting.

A grain truck has lost its load
Spilling, dusting, making slippery the road,
Crunchy underfoot.
The wiry wreck of a truck tyre twists black,
Its rubbered pieces littering, strewn.

Road crews in shorts with wide-brimmed hats sweat
As they re-sheet the pavement with flashing monsters.
It steams and flicks up sticky black gravel
Pocking my car,
Threatening the windscreen.

The radio lists the fires, alerts.

A steel train pierces the stubble:
A dried out Roberts, an even drier Williams,
Here's another bushfire – its heat has melted the tar
And here's another road crew, replacing crumpled crash bars;
Even the sandstone in the cuttings looks hot,
The drab scrub wilting, withering.

It's going to be a long, hot summer.

Russell Drysdale was an Australian modernist artist famous for his distinctive vision of the Australian outback and drought in the 1940s and 50s.

Parrots in the Pears

Newstead, Mullaley, NSW

Green parrots feast on the old orchard's pears,
Their dainty claws and quiet determination
Contrasting oddly with the spits of the pips.
The local radio plays
And the mixer putters on.

The rooster all puffed up in the heat crows.

Julia takes the motorbike down to move the cows:
Max sprints through the stubble – wow is he fast! – then
    loops around;
Tui follows, while Kipper trundles along behind the wheel.
Rufus, suddenly left behind, splays his back legs, takes off,
And dashes down to join them, straight through the hole in
    the fence.

Treed volcanic mounds lump the horizon.

The parrots are back.
Three wrens hop about looking for leftovers.
The rooster crows again.
Here come the cows – hard along the fence –
Coralled by the dogs and the bike.

The rooster crows again.

The flies keep bugging me
And there are all these strange black insects.
It's hot. 44.5 degrees.
And the air conditioner is broken.

The dogs seem to bounce.
Racing
Tails straight out behind.

The parrots have light green undersides
And yellow edgings on their tails,
Red underwing, and a vibrant blue on their backs,
Seen only in flight.
They give a high-pitched squeak.

The shovel scrapes the barrow.
When the mixer stops I'll know it's time for tea.

The cows are almost running now. Huddled.

A king parrot has joined the greens –
Orange breast with blue-green wing.
Now there's two.
They're noisy and aggressive, fighting over food.
See them grab that pear and twist.

The mixer stops. It's time for tea.
Job done. Day done.
Time for food.

Glen Ayr, Pokolbin

for the kids: to be read aloud, engagingly

Locusts shrill in the gums along the creek
Electronic torture pulsing with the heat
Black cockies caw the coming of the storm
Kookaburras cheer the wormy wet of dawn.

Pardalotes feed babies screeching in the eaves
Taking their turns, watching for thieves
Geckos walk the ceiling, dash about the walls
Spiders weave their sticky traps, then hide in woven balls.

Goanna sniffs the garbage, waddles down the track
Grandpa dispatches the red-belly black
Lizards sneak inside and slide across the floor
Their give-away tails poke under the door.

Wrens play in fountains, pools from a pipe,
Darting and wagging, blue satin bright
A tawny frogmouth impossible to see
Blends into branches, an ironbark tree.

A tortoise braves the traffic, his long neck twists around
A fox struts unchallenged – he considers all his ground
A rabbit bobs its white tail, running though the green
Beware the fox! – he'll sneak and pounce – you'll soon be
 tasty feed.

Goanna smells a barbecue, poking out his head
Only trouble is – he's under a bed!
Frightened by the screams of a naked guest
He shreds all the curtains and makes himself a pest.

Eagles glide above, catching prey upon the wing,
Magpies call a chorus, butcherbirds sing,
Roos bounce majestic, alert across the view
What a gift Glen Ayr is: this open-range zoo!

Falling in Love with Queensland

Mum and Dad had their first holiday away from us kids in
    Queensland:
Karumba and Normanton.
I still remember their fresh return,
followed by that favourite family treasure, the crocodile:
long-snouted, with marble eye and vicious teeth –
ideal for scaring naïve American visitors
and wayward sons of English gents
who think we're still colonials.

Soon too we played round pools at Surfers,
strode the line between states an hour apart,
learned stories of lost planes in the Lamington, sucking
    Buderim ginger
and rode the waves at Noosa.

The first holiday on my own was with a school group at the
    age of 9 –
too young, on reflection,
midst homesick sobs and letters never sent.
We flew to Proserpine and caught the boat from Shute Harbour
to Long Island in the Whitsundays,
staying in cabins filled with mozzies,
veiled on coconut shores.

Each day we discovered a new cove, a new island, like pirates:
Hayman, Lindeman, Daydream
treasure
trawling, swimming,
trekking through jungled palms
with viney tripping ropes and matted clinging ferns,
Our yacht was even lifted, rolled, by a grey-white whale shark
the fishing boats had tracked
all the way down the coast from T.I. –
that's when I really fell in love with Queensland.

As teenagers, we flew the milk run to Cloncurry:
Townsville, Charters, Hughenden, Julia Creek,
landing in a locust plague, splatting all the glass;
by Jeep south to Dad's leases, sleeping under stars,
the tiny pub showing off its dinosaur bones,
Doc Morrison hypnotising Sandy, who ended up in tears,
the house with sack doors, dirt floors
and the toothless old-timer who, after some while,
attended to this impediment
by digging out his teeth from gritty pockets,
to wide-eyed stares from us all.

The other house in town:
Mum and her three boys, all over 50,
with three sets of matching workwear drying on the line,
owned a stack of leases –
mining each metal as the market moved –
were thus raking in the dough,
though you'd never know.

That night, amidst the blackboys camped abed the creek
our host told us one of the pubs in Isa would be fired –
and it was.

Dad had other interests up on the Tableland:
Moly, Wolfram,
hacked from flaky, steely veins flowing underground.
What fun we had donning hard hats
and braving the cage to dripping damp vaults of burrows below,
spooky in their vastness.
One of the Yugoslav groups used to train in those rugged
    bushy ranges
not unlike home
and blew up a bridge!
discovered Monday morning by miners
no doubt glad of an excuse for a hangover holiday.

That country's littered with old airstrips –
army leftovers from tented war cities
'mongst the tobacco;
we discovered one quite by chance and had great laughs
zooming up and down the weedy concrete runway
with Mum screaming,
'Stop it, David. You'll kill us all!'

Whale shark: rhincodon typus, the largest extant fish species.
T.I.: Thursday Island.
Blackboys: grass trees.

Rock Climbing

There's one very important rule about rock climbing:
Tell your mother the day after.

A Man's Frown

It's in a man's frown
is his beauty.

Doha, Qatar

The wall of heat hits hard
as I descend the steps
and search for space on the bus.
Doesn't it even cool down at midnight?
An open oven: ever radiating.
How could anybody ever live here?
Flashing orange lights twinkle in the dark,
moving as a massive trainset
round unseen rails.
Planes are lined up,
neatly parked,
like toys in a kid's game –
all grey and maroon, with oryx-antlered tails.

From the four corners of the globe they've come
to pour forth their cargo
into the giant sorting machine of the terminal –
only for all to be churned out again –
a monstrous pulsating breathing hub:
in and out, in and out –
will my bag ever find me?
Through the window, the regular passing of long-necked beasts,
overhead, their regular roar –
the breathy voice of Arabic,
its back-to-front script,
the burkas and the skullcaps
all tell me
I've landed in an other world,
a passing through the desert,
a gargantuan tent –
only the camels have turned into planes.

Trocadero Gardens, Paris

La Tour towers over ordered avenues
Montparnasse a squat black candle behind its steely flame
Les Invalides gleams gold
Longest light this summer's night.

I sit among the sculptures: classic stone
My citron pressé sour yet sweet
Well-dressed kids do one-eighties on their blades
And roll a dance with friends, clunking backwards down the steps.

The linden trees waft sweet
Even the gangs are groomed
The tourists take their Japanese photos
Raising their arms in make-believe suspension – or is it praise?

The world meets here,
Including a Tuareg shawled in white:
Engineers built this city, with art
And tell above our glory of a wonder long forgot.

La Tour: better known in English as the Eiffel Tower.

Montparnasse: its 59-floor monolithic dominance occasioning the banning of skyscrapers in Paris.

Les Invalides: military monument and burial site of Napoleon Bonaparte.

iBagel, Copenhagen

Isra takes my order with a modest, gentle smile,
his head-dressed sister beside making bagel sandwiches
    with curry, pesto or crème fraîche dressing.
The menu's all in English, though most order in Danish.
There's gelato italiano in the display case,
    as well as McDonald's pastries and donuts
    and teas from Numi and the London Tea Company.
You can order online and use the wi-fi
but, best of all, there are beautiful books
spilling from the shelves
in a feast of languages: Spanish, Swedish, Arabic –
all obviously read.

Somewhere over Turkey

Somewhere over Turkey
an earnest young boy throws a mat at my feet,
makes some movement cross his chest
and kneels in prayer,
bowing his head seven times.

I close my eyes and pray for him silently.

Herceg-Novi Summer Suite

I A Man's World

Morning and evening, morning and evening
The ferries ply the strait
From Kamenari to Lepitani
From Lepitani to Kamenari
Always ready, always waiting
In smart orange freshly painted.

With flags flying proudly
They shoulder their heavy loads gently
Tankers sit as toys on the deck
The bus passengers stretching their legs are but flies.

Every car, bus and truck
Crosses here
On their way down, on their way back
Every girl, every mate
Passes through – sealed with a shake
All is seen, all is shown
By their plates they are known.

A deckhand starting his shift
Arrives in shorts
And cannot help but tie the ropes.
He disappears, and emerges
Proud in his uniform of blue and white striped shirt
And navy overalls with fluoro strips.

It's a man's world here.
Casual, alert, and ruled.
It works, and is glad.

Morning and evening, morning and evening
The ferries ply the strait
From Kamenari to Lepitani
From Lepitani to Kamenari
Always ready, always waiting
In smart orange freshly painted.

II The Passing Parade: Breakfast on the Šetalište Pet Danica

I sit beside the walkway,
watching the haze on the blue,
beside my chair a passing stream,
all brought by the bay below.

Mums and dads with toddlers,
lilos, prams and toys,
sulky youths,
severely shorn,
old soldiers in their speedos –
flaps hanging, unadorned.

> The brimming boats make their crossings to the beaches outside,
> While a bloke with a megaphone advertises something from a dinghy puttering along the shore,
> The Swiss most organised read their guide,
> The waiter chalks up the daily specials,
> A fat boy strips his sausage of its skin,
> A slamming door means the delivery van has arrived and all hands appear for its unloading,
> A family exchanges sultry lines,
> Two men on their phones catch every passing bikini.

A gang of late risers all lanky,
healthy, athletic and slim,
swing by, self-consciously casual,
enjoying the sun on their skin.

The 'new cool' slashed by their man-bags,
earnestly make for the beach,
while the locals carry their towels rolled,
swarthy, necked with sharks' teeth.

    A boy eagerly bounces his ball,
    Two lads emerge at the pizzeria,
    their untowelled bodies glistening.

    A crippled boy slides by,
    Brave in the heat and the sun,
    O Lord, give him joy in the morning,
    when this world of shadow is done.

III At Kamenari: Olympics 2012

Here I am enjoying a quiet drink,
watching the ferries load,
sitting obliviously under the TV
churning out something in a language foreign.
Next I know a kid all limbs
wearing nothing but blue swimmers with Serbia slashed across them,
waving a red and gold Montenegro towel,
has gathered his mates
and I'm facing a crowd all skin cheering on the water polo.

IV Water Polo Training: Montenegro Juniors

Sixteen dark heads hug the wall
The whistle blows and half lunge out
The whistle blows again
The other half follow fast
Up and back, up and back
Too long to count –
They're strong these boys
And this is why –
The whistle blows again
Throws in threes, twists and twirls
All right hands bar one
The goals go in
The caps go on –
This is why they're here –
It's tough and hard
And sharp and strong
Some get swaps but most play long –
The goalies never change.

It's warm-down time
And cross the pool they float
One arm held high
It waves and shakes –
A merman fin:
Quicker than a goalie's save.

V In the Garden Restoran, Perast

In the Garden Restoran,
looking down the fjord with salt on skin,
the scattered tables display their guests.

In one corner the French lads in muscle shirts
devour a pizza with girls in tow.
In another, my shirtless photofriend from the boat
sits with his girlfriend and mother-in-law enjoying a smoke.
Beside the orange and gold summer daisies
two women share a pancake dripping with cream
and a red-haired couple with toddlers verging on sunstroke
search anxiously for some shade.

On one side of the chugging cake fridge
two tall Serbian sisters
sit with their restless lanky boys
waiting for their hairy husbands in speedos
to anchor their boat.

On the other, a frail English grandcouple
enjoy the view through sunglasses
with a flock of delicate girls preserving their complexions
under wide-brimmed hats
and flowing sleeved dresses to the ground.

How on earth did they ever survive in Australia?

VI Day Trip to Žanjic

The cove describes a classic arc,
its water clear.
Yachts are moored outside the swimming net,
its orange and white floaters cutting a neat line,
joining the shores.

I choose the coolest spot on the beach,
leaning against an ancient stone wall
under some thatched shade.

The boats, with legs all overhanging their sides,
come and go from the short pier,
unloading and reloading the day's sun-seekers.
Even the cops are here in black zodiacs.
Swimmers loll in the water,
Snorkellers explore,
four boys practise their throws at the water-polo net,
while two others hang around, eager to join.

A collection of heads bobs across the bay,
yellow paddle-boats muck about the net,
with shrieks and giggles in the air.
Two wet boys limb their way up the boat launch.

The beach is pattern striped with umbrellas right down to the
 water:
Niksic green, Frikom blue, red and white Amstel Light.
On the walkway behind,
another patterned line – all beer –
this time in cobalt blues.
Up the hill, gnarled-trunk olives and clay-tiled roofs
archive and reveal generations of family holidays.

Pajo, with its white floater side-protectors has returned.
She blows her whistle for our jaunt to the Blue Cave
and the crumbling old fort on Mamula,
its cavernous tunnels, crafted masonry and high ramparts
delighting, evoking
medieval empires and pirates – centuries –
midst the whales and the dolphins,
the salt and the sun.

With thanks to Anne Elder, *Regattas*.

VII The Ballet on the Bay

I sit beside the walkway,
The wash of the bay below,
The day has died, the breeze relieves,
Time for this evening's show.

They enter from stage right and left,
Sometimes fast with a quickened step –
Lads with a goal in mind –
Sometimes slow, ambling along,
Parents with toddlers in tow.

The band plays golden oldies
And a pencil-thin Montenegrin in six-inch heels
Sings Tina Turner and 'Hotel California' in Serbian.

The pizzeria glows behind,
With the perky girl waiting for trade –
Its neon sign strobes the night –
While on the other side
Four blokes argue over the fish
And a kid with glasses and his dad
Eye off the gelati display.

A bunch of youths enjoying their shirtless torsos,
With boardies low on the hips,
Rustles by;
Strollers, dogs, oldies,
A woman carrying a plastic horse
Won as a prize at the fair,
Even more lanky Montenegrin beauties
In even higher heels,
A flock of plaited girls,
Locals out for the shops –
Cool and clunky,
Alert and dreamy,
They're all here
This summer night
Watching
And unwatching
The ballet on the bay.

VIII You're Never Sure or Nobody Speaks English

You're always a little anxious leaving the old Iron Curtain
 countries:
You're never sure if they'll let you out,
or, more likely, if you'll be able to get out,
or if at that last moment you'll be quietly passed into an
 airport room
to end up, forgotten, with a motley strew of leftovers
no one knows what to do with –
And nobody speaks English.

It's 5 a.m. and I take one last breath of the bay.
Rain is softly falling.
The umbrellas are folded below, the beach chairs lined up
 empty.
I lug my suitcase down and up the steps
and have to leave the hotel door unlocked if I'm to leave the key.
The taxi is not there.
I wait, disbelieving.
I start walking in the rain and two arrive!
And nobody speaks English.
The seat belt doesn't work.

The bus station is already full with red-eyed passengers
and one snoring bus driver in what could be my bus.
I stow my bag beneath and board in faith.
The old soldier eventually stirs and we leave right on time.

The clean light of dawn shows off the bay as the locals walk
 to work.
The ferry line is full of cars in the bus lane,
already full with two coaches and some minivans.
Our hearts sink,
but by nosing between queues and barging in
we make the second ferry.
Thank God everyone knows the word for airport,
but I'm anxious the driver doesn't take off before I've
 collected my bag from below –
What on earth's the word for bag?

The airport is chock full of long lines with all the signs out.
I wait to find I'm in the Leningrad line when I arrive at the
 counter.
Another queue.
The place is teeming with Russians – 17 out of 20 flights
 when the boards come good.
And nobody speaks English.

The security line stretches across the whole length of the
    terminal –
a human wall blocking everybody else trying to come in.
On the other side the place is packed, with not a bite nor a
    drink to be found.
I try my stale sandwich, but my empty stomach cannot bear it.
I discover grease from the bus all over my trousers.
Our plane is an old Fokker hired for the season with no
    markings –
I probably flew in it as a kid.
The Russian flights are all delayed.

You're always a little anxious when leaving the old Iron
    Curtain countries:
you're never sure if they'll let you out,
or, more likely, if you'll be able to get out.

We're on the tarmac.
The rugged mountains overhang.
The fire trucks are vintage Soviet, as is the aged tractor
    pulling the stairs.
The crew includes a tall Tinkerbell with blonde hair – classic
    Montenegro.
I can see I'm going to miss it already.

Herceg-Novi, Montenegro, August 2012.

At the British Museum

Somewhere in Mesopotamia 4000 BC
I began to think of ancient cities, with streets
and writing and irrigation
and cylinder seals in fine détail
and wondered at our arrogance
in dismissing Abraham and Moses
as myth for the modern mind.

If I were Abraham I'd weep at holocaustic horrors
cycling through the years
and pray the promise for his heirs
of hope through lonely tears.

Lament for Podgorica: Isaiah 55

O Podgorica, city of Romans and Turks
Your paths are in pieces, your gardens unmown
Your communist concrete crumbles and rusts
Can you yet dream of a hope still unknown?

O Podgorica, city of tumbledown walls
The ruins of sad empires leave their ugly stain
Your weathered old men mooch around dead monuments
Can you but grieve for a dream now forlorn?

O Podgorica, centre of others more fine
What have you to look forward to?
Where and how will you shine?

O Podgorica, look over your shoulder no more
Your rivers run free
Your boys jump and swim
Your long-legged beauties are strong
Grasp hold of your hope
Make Him your own
And the mountains will sing to the sea.

Podgorica (population 186,000) is the capital and largest city of Montenegro. Situated at a major crossroads between east and west, at the confluence of the Ribnica and Morača Rivers, it has been settled by many, including the Illyrians, Greeks, Romans, Slavs and Ottomans. Occupied by Austria-Hungary during World War I and heavily bombed and razed in World War II, it served under the name of Titograd as capital of Montenegro in the former Yugoslavia, until Montenegro gained independence in 2006. Unlike most of Montenegro, which is ruggedly mountainous, Podgorica lies centrally in a mainly flat plain, with extremely hot and dry summers, untempered by the breezes found on the coast.

Rendition: On Hearing News of American Torture

Oh America! Mother of freedom and law
How has it come to this?
This fire's blown back
Searing, ashing your mouth
How can you now speak? –
Your hands are soiled.
Where others stoop, you have no need to tread
You have a gospel heart, or had,
Till quickly doused, waterboarded away
In chilling holocaustic calm – top down
Managed, filmed, by doctors, lawyers, worlds apart
Betraying law to serve your bullying needs.

Who gave you the right to rule in other men's domains,
While in your own farce law to make?
Winners do not their victims' freedoms take
Lest having took they lose the very freedoms fought;
Forgiveness finds friends, bitterness eats away
How one treats one's enemies will soon be mirrored home
Heed carefully lest you soon be naked, tortured and despised:
Animals are kinder to their foes.
If you are free, or freedom make,
Fight this battle with the heart
What's done in secret bears no honour less its telling tells its good
This telling tells its shame; more shame to come, I fear
Till this festered wound is cleansed
And righteousness is won.

Esther

for Kate, Anna and Xanthe

She stakes her neck to plead her cause
Her people's life is on the brim
Her whole life was planned for this
And in her rescue points to Him.
This amazing mirrored tale
Makes the first the last the first
Lifts the low, makes low the high
Makes all reign who choose to die.

King for King

Reflections prompted by 2 Samuel 11:1–12:7 and Romans 8:33–34
With thanks to Tim Keller

What gracious steal
To call the king
Judging on his throne;
No friend to save
The King of Kings
Who makes all sin his own.

Behold the man
Who'll judge the judge
Accept his cup of thorns;
With grace he pleads
Forgiveness now
His righteous robe adorns.

This king did fight
In battle led
Stood aside his throne;
No sin to call
No friend to plead
He pleads the sin of all.

Be Strong and Courageous

for Rod West: Joshua 1:9

When I tread the verge of Jordan
bid my anxious fears subside;
death of death, and hell's destruction,
land me safe on Canaan's side:
songs of praises, songs of praises,
I will ever give to thee,
I will ever give to thee.

Oh Rod!
How surreal to be planning your funeral
while you're as sharp as a tack, alert
remembering names and people;
how can I thank you enough
for all the remembrances that come flooding back:
the long hours chatting at midnight in your study,
the Latin classes, house plays, Bible Studies and early
    morning chapel services,
even when you lost your temper over some unknown mistake –
thereby evidencing your love –
the hard work building the Greek Theatre
among gum trees
with bush stone laboriously hewn and carted
Oh the folly of it!
yet the glory! – soon envied –
the undistracted vision and determination
'One swallow doesn't make a summer'
the commitment to the idea, the principle, the ancient art,

the care for Janet and the kids
and for all the wild boys
you fear you've hurt
in your enthusiastic clumsiness –
the frank awareness of your youth.

Yet God
yet God takes your very breaks
and makes a strength
and makes a life

Thank God He gave us a long afternoon
uninterrupted
to talk about old times, people, and the certain hope of heaven;
you've said all these prayers over many years
and always believed them,
but now they flow with precious power
and bring a holy balm;
be strong and courageous
as you fight this final fight:
the Promised Land awaits –
safe in the Shepherd's arms.

Superscription from 'Guide Me, O Thou Great Jehovah', William
Williams, 1762, trans. Peter Williams, 1771

Greenland Quartet

I Attiak Ittuk crosses the Arctic Circle

In rolling waves the ship ploughs on
Foam across her hardened prow
Lonely in an icy sea
Eyes peeled wide for whale's white blow.

The distant shore more distant moves
Its jagged snow mounts lost in cloud
Not a seagull braves the freeze
As northward pushes King of Seas.

Maniitsoq is mild to this
Kangaamiut a coloured cove
All those north more dogged brave
Midst calving glaciers, black dark days.

One translation of Attiak Ittuk is King of Seas. North of the Arctic Circle, working dogs are commonly used, and these are occasionally bred with wolves. In order to keep the breed untainted, any dogs that travel south of the circle cannot return.

II Morning, Attiak Ittuk

I draw my morning's curtain
to discover the porthole
filled with an iceberg:
snowy white diamond,
sharp and angle-edged,
shimmering blue.

III Sailing with Icebergs, Eki Glacier

With eyes alert, Aviaq Ittuk rumbles along,
threading her way through floating white islands,
electric blues:
planed long and fluffy flat,
sharp and jagged angled,
bridges, tunnels, smooth-ribbed contours,
sea-sculptured through ever-changing disappearing forms,
till seas themselves renew.

IV With an Amazing View

What I really love doing
is ordinary, everyday things
like towelling off, getting dressed, eating breakfast,
reading the Bible and writing poetry
with an amazing view.

Tromsø Quartet

I View from a Hotel Window, Tromsø

The picture postcard landscape sits clear,
backed by the forest green of summer snowed peaks
with rows of red-roofed houses along the contours of their feet.
The glinting waters of the fjord stretch across,
motor boats foam past,
Two fishing boats set out all optimistically,
The bridge in its graceful arc rises to the left,
while the Arctic Cathedral in its slices of white
stands watch proudly like a landed iceberg on the other shore.
The *Hurtigruten* slides past,
her rose-red stripe a cummerbund between the black hull,
    white decks.
A sky diver hangs in the air, winging his way smoothly to
    land on the green,
and here's another, like an oversized orange seagull,
and still another, yellow this time, and yet another,
who somehow manages to fly high, silhouetted against the
    cloudless blue –
a double view: mirrored all in the hotel's other wing.

Hurtigruten: The Norwegian coastal ferry, carrying both passengers and freight, and, increasingly, tourists.

II The Cloudy Finger

The cloudy finger
weaves its misty way up the fjord
between the jagged snowied peaks:
silently, lightly,
wrapping the bridge,
filling the bay,
gathering in the pretty wooded houses along the gentle shores,
till shrouding all.

Then, a harsh microphoned voice
tells me the *Hurtigruten* has arrived
somewhere in the mist.
Her lights appear – burning the fog,
revealing her white stern, or is it her bow,
nestled in the haloes
from the lamps along the pier?

III Crossing the Bridge

Yesterday, when I tried to cross the bridge to the Arctic Cathedral,
I made it halfway up,
but then the sight at my feet of the water far below –
despite the high steel fence,
the strong rail,
and all I told and willed myself –
produced in me such a strong reaction
that I couldn't take a step further.

Do people jump off bridges due to this?
Is this why Kathy and Pa can't fly?
And why Uncle Adrian now says he has vertigo?
Is this my genes, my rock climbing days, too much sodium,
or just turning old?

IV Through Famine and Fire

What is it about Norwegians and museums?
There are so many of them.
Is it the cold and dry, preserving paper and artefacts?
Is it in their genes, to sort and stow?
Or is it in their faith?
Knowing that a good God has brought them thus far
Through famine and fire:
Remember Him.

Trio: Return to Oslo

I Oslofjord, Early Morning

The ferry is still now.
Sliding up the fjord,
She follows a twin loaded with containers,
After rolling, squirming in the strait.
Fresh light shines on glowing white walls
Of trimmed-neat summer cottages,
Bearing their pennants proudly
Through the pines.

A mill glides by – its woodchip mountains growing
Beside a dockside crane loading stacks of belted timber
Into a sinking hull.
The sea is glass.
A trawler passes, a yacht, a quarry,
A red and white striped mini-marker bu'oy.
'Not a bad way to spend a morning,' my tablemate drawls,
'Not a bad way, indeed.'

An island with four grey cannon poking out of a stone fort
Shelters a harbour of canoe coves.
A pencil case of masts signals a distant marina.

Our sliding stills.
We float.
Nudged into the quayside,
Roped fast,
Before disgorging our clanking cargo
Into this capital city,
Settled on the sound.

II View from a Breakfast Window, Oslo

The Oslo Boat sits large and square, emptying her clanking cargo,
The Opera's white marble glistens, its angles melting into the sea,
The sky is cloud, with drizzling rain making slippery the paths,
And the banners flap furl in the breeze.

The tourists tread carefully as they climb the Opera roof, umbrellas in hand,
A solo figure in orange fluoro stands watch on the German frigate –
I discover later it's just a safety suit, but perhaps it does the job just as well –
A heritage boat sails past, her canvas covers shrouding her load,
And the grey grim fog sets in, drenching my day.

The B-doubles appearing from the boat creep crawl around the roadworks, sniffing their way,
The buses all gleaming with headlights on also mooch through the gloom,
their sides painted with interesting names from right across the continent, which I squint to discern,
The fort, with shining gold roof keeps guard,
The mountains surround,
Cradling
This wealthy Wellington
Emerging from the mist.

III Vigeland Park Revisited: Summer Evening

The colonnades of maple trees smell sweet and cool
Water plays from the fountains, sits fresh beneath the bridge
The lake is lawned with picnics, frisbees and bare-chested
    torsoed youths
Playing kickball cross a rope tied between trees.

Vigeland's statues line the paths, mount the crest:
A dad carries his kids – one under each arm
A boy holds his brother on his head
A father playlifts his toddler:
Muscled, athletic, lean.

A mother cradles her baby at the breast
Two brothers standing look skywards
Another mother holds her little one outstretched
A couple dance, arms lifted high:
Bronzed-blue green.

A man tumbles his daughter, her plaits falling:
A grandpa takes his grandson for a stroll
Two boys wrestle with their father, nearly pulling out his hair
A bunch of girls stand gathered in secret conference
A couple kiss.

Life in all its cycles
Wondrous in its story
Granites, sparkling bronzes
In vital virile glory.

www.ingramcontent.com/pod-product-compliance
Lightning Source LLC
Chambersburg PA
CBHW070050120526
44589CB00034B/1687